MI ABUELO CÉSAR

Written by
Eduardo Chávez

Illustrated by
Evelyn Barajas

Copyright © 2025 by Eduardo Chávez

All rights reserved. No part of this publication may be reproduced, stored in a retrieval system, or transmitted in any form or by any means—electronic, mechanical, photocopying, recording, or otherwise—without the prior written permission of the publisher, except in the case of brief quotations used in reviews or articles.

Illustrations by Evelyn Barajas
Edited by Crystal Watanabe
Book designed by Annie Wilkinson

Published in the United States by Latindia Studios LLC

Hardback ISBN: 979-8-218-76904-8

Printed in the United States of America

For more information, visit: **eduardomchavez.com**

For Mami

As I walk down the street with my dad in San Francisco, a bright, colorful mural of my abuelo César Chávez catches my eye.

His soft smile and peaceful eyes watch over the neighborhood.

Beaming with curiosity and a little nervousness, I wonder to myself, Who was this man? Could I ever be like him?

"Papá, why is Abuelo César so famous?" I ask.

"What did he do?"

"Your abuelo César was a farmworker,

an activist,

and a labor organizer," my dad says.

I think I know what farmworkers do, but I have never heard of the other two jobs. "What's an activist and labor organizer, Papá?"

An activist is someone who stands up for what is right, and an organizer helps bring people together to make their community a better place," my dad explains.

"Your abuelo César did both."

I picture my abuelo passionately speaking in front of a crowd. He didn't just work in the fields, he helped change the world.

Could I ever do something this big?

"Farmworkers are some of the hardest-working people in our society," my dad says. "We depend on them for the fresh fruits and vegetables we eat."

Listening to my dad, I take a deep breath, feeling the cool California breeze on my skin. I can almost taste the juicy fruits just thinking about them.

"Why did Abuelo César become an activist and organizer if he was a farmworker, too?" I ask, my curiosity growing.

My dad smiles. "Let's go see. I think you'll understand better when you work the fields for yourself."

In the fields, farmworkers pick red grapes off the vine. I watch with amazement at how quickly they work in the cold and foggy Northern California weather.

It looks hard!

I bend down and pick some grapes myself, just like the other workers.

At first the cold doesn't bother me.

But as time passes, my fingers and lower back begin to stiffen.

In awe of how difficult this work is, I wonder, How do farmworkers do this every single day?

My dad nods. "Your abuelo César picked fruits and vegetables when he was only a little older than you, and so did I.

When I was twelve, I picked cherries to help support my family."

I look at him with surprise.

"I didn't know you were a farmworker, Papá."

"Yes, you come from a family of proud farmworkers, Eduardo," he says.

"Chicanos have done this work for many years. These are your roots."

My heart feels full as I imagine my abuelo and dad working in the fields.

This important work is in my family's history. I feel like I am a part of something bigger than myself.

"Is that why Abuelo César wanted to help the farmworkers?"

My dad nods again. "He saw for himself how hard the work was and wanted to make things better.

That's why he and Dolores Huerta started a union for farmworkers called the United Farm Workers."

"What's a union, Papá?" I ask.

"A union is an organization that represents and supports workers by requiring fair pay for their labor, and safe working conditions," he explains.

Hearing this, I finally understand why my abuelo César is so important to history.

He made his dream come true of a world where farmworkers are treated fairly.

My back straightens as a great sense of pride fills me. I am proud to be Chicano.

With the ache in my lower back and thoughts of the fields in my mind, I go to school, excited yet nervous. I can't wait to share my abuelo César's story and the importance of farmworkers with my classmates.

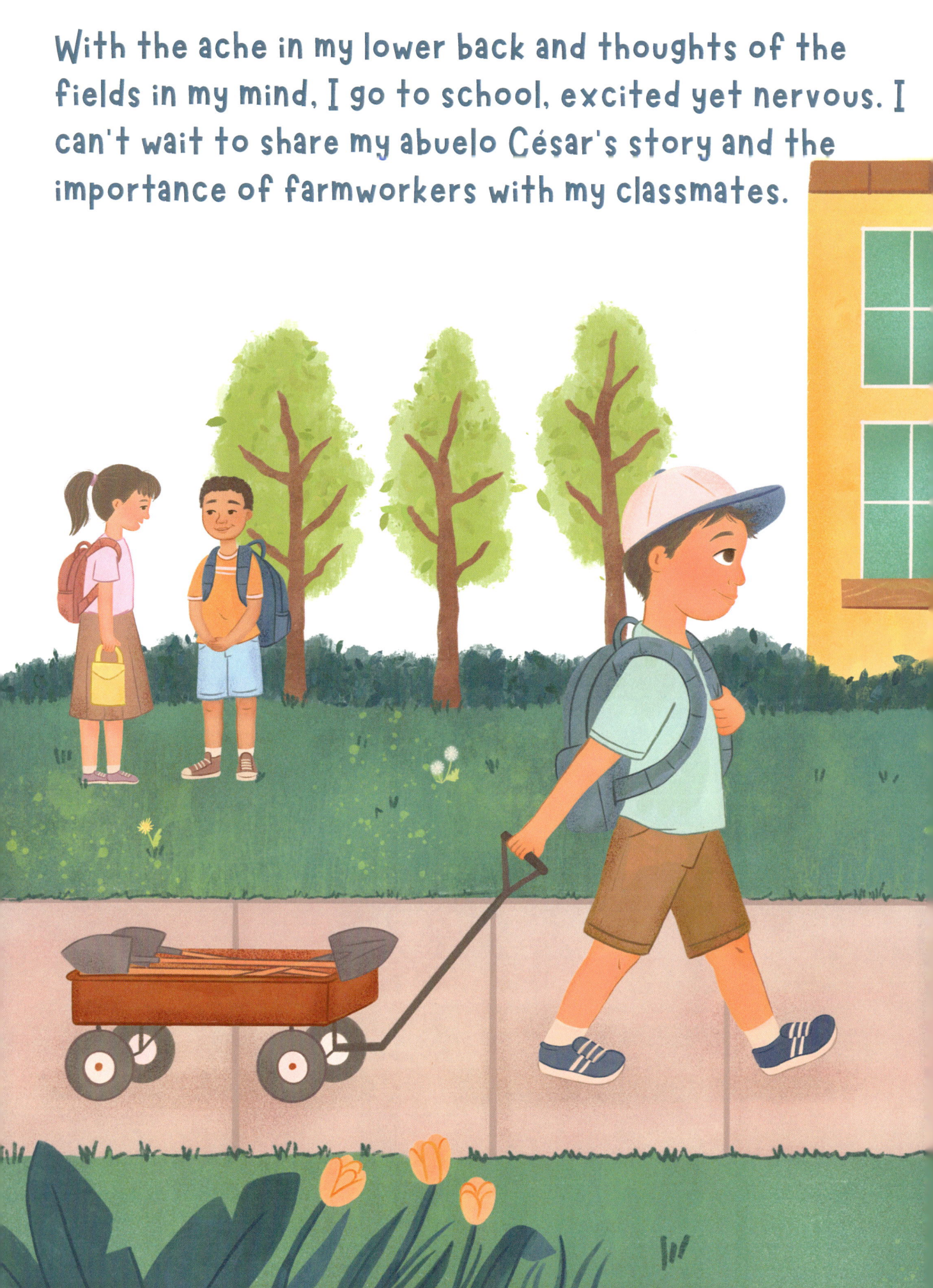

Hopefully they will understand why farmworkers are so significant to our country and beyond.

At school, my dad helps me organize an activity with my classmates. I have everyone pick up a shovel and show them what it felt like when I visited the fields.

As my classmates bend over and dig in the ground, I explain, "This is the kind of work farmworkers do every single day. They are some of the most important people we have in this country. They feed us."

At the end of my presentation, with confidence I say, "My name is Eduardo Chávez, and my abuelo was César Chávez. I come from a family of Chicano farmworkers, and we are proud of our roots. It is up to us to keep my abuelo's legacy of helping others alive.

He showed us the way. Now we must follow the path. Sí, se puede!"

As my classmates cheer, I smile. I know who I am and I know what I stand for.

Just like my abuelo César, we can all do our part to make the world a better place.

My grandfather and me, 1992

www.ingramcontent.com/pod-product-compliance
Lightning Source LLC
Chambersburg PA
CBRC091205010526
44107CB00021B/1249